4/13
F

D1029584

SUPER SILLY
SCIENCE
JOKES

Creepy, Crawly Jokes About Spiders and Other Bugs

Laugh and Learn About Science

Written by Melissa Stewart
Illustrated by Gerald Kelley

Enslow Elementary, an imprint of Enslow Publishers, Inc.

Enslow Elementary is a registered trademark of Enslow Publishers, Inc.

Library of Congress Cataloging-in-Publication Data
Stewart, Melissa.
  Creepy, crawly jokes about spiders and other bugs : laugh and learn about science / written by
Melissa Stewart ; illustrated by Gerald Kelley.
      p. cm. — (Super silly science jokes)
  Includes index.
  Summary: "Learn about a variety of bugs including true bugs, beetles, moths, and bees. Read jokes
about them, and learn how to write your own"—Provided by publisher.
  ISBN 978-0-7660-3966-7
  1. Insects—Juvenile literature. 2. Arthropoda—Juvenile literature. 3. Insects—Humor.
4. Arthropoda—Humor. I. Kelley, Gerald, ill II. Title.
  QL467.2.S7765 2013
  595.702'07—dc23
                                    2011026526

Future editions:

Paperback ISBN 978-1-4644-0167-1

ePUB ISBN 978-1-4645-1074-8

PDF ISBN 978-1-4646-1074-5

Printed in China

012012 Leo Paper Group, Heshan City, Guangdong, China

10 9 8 7 6 5 4 3 2 1

To Our Readers: We have done our best to make sure all Internet Addresses in this book were
active and appropriate when we went to press. However, the author and the publisher have no
control over and assume no liability for the material available on those Internet sites or on other Web
sites they may link to. Any comments or suggestions can be sent by e-mail to comments@enslow.com
or to the address on the back cover.

Illustration Credits: © 2011 Gerald Kelley (www.geraldkelley.com)

Photo Credits: © 2011 Photos.com, a division of Getty Images, pp. 16, 27, 32; Enslow Publishers,
Inc., p. 46; Eye of Science/Photo Researchers, Inc., p. 24; Shutterstock.com, pp. 4, 7, 8, 11, 12, 15,
19, 20, 23, 28, 31, 35, 36, 38, 39, 40, 43.

Cover Illustration: © 2011 Gerald Kelley (www.geraldkelley.com)

Enslow Elementary
an imprint of
Enslow Publishers, Inc.
40 Industrial Road
Box 398
Berkeley Heights, NJ 07922
USA
http://www.enslow.com

Contents

What a Bug!

Here's some news that might surprise you: All insects are bugs, but not all bugs are insects!

Confused? Don't be. An insect is one kind of bug. It has three main body parts—a head, a **thorax**, and an **abdomen**. It has six legs and a hard **exoskeleton** covering its body.

Spiders aren't insects. Neither are ticks, mites, millipedes, or centipedes. But according to the dictionary, all of these little, creepy crawly critters are bugs.

This book will teach you all kinds of cool facts about bugs. But that's not all. This book is also chock full of jokes. Some of them will make you laugh out loud. Others might make you groan. (Sorry.) But either way, you'll have a good time.

Q: What do "spiders" and "insects" have in common?

A: Both words have seven letters.

Q: Why do bedbugs think they are the prettiest insects?

A: They get plenty of beauty sleep.

True Bugs

Okay, let's review. The dictionary says that spiders and centipedes, mites and millipedes are all bugs. But guess what? Scientists don't agree. They use the word "bug" in a very different way. And that really is confusing. In fact, it could drive you buggy.

When scientists say "bug" or "true bug," they're talking about a specific group of insects. Stink bugs. Giant water bugs. Bed bugs. They're all true bugs.

What do these insects have in common? A beak with sucking mouthparts. It is attached to the front of the insect's head. Most true bugs carry their wings crossed over their backs. The wings overlap to make an "X." And many true bugs are shaped like a shield. They have broad "shoulders" and a narrow tail.

Q: What's an insect's favorite dance?

A: The jitterbug.

forest bug

Q: What did the backswimmer bug
look for when it got tired?

A: A water boatman bug.

7

Beetles

ladybug

You might guess that a ladybug is a true bug. But it's not. It's a beetle. And it isn't alone. One-third of all the insects alive today are beetles. So far, scientists have named more than 350,000 kinds, or **species**, of beetles. And there are millions more left to discover.

Why are there so many beetles on Earth? Because they can live almost anywhere—from snowy mountaintops to hot, dry deserts. Some beetles live in fast-flowing streams. Others spend all their time underground.

A beetle has two pairs of wings. A heavy, armored exoskeleton protects it from enemies. Powerful mouthparts grab, bite, and chew all kinds of food—from leaves and seeds to dead animals and rotting **dung**. Eew! Gross!

Q: What kind of beetle has no trouble seeing in the dark?

A: A lightning bug.

Q: Where do young beetles go on Saturday nights?

A: To the grub club.

4 Butterflies and Moths

How many kinds of butterflies live on Earth? About 18,000 species. But that's nothing compared to the number of moths. Some scientists think 250,000 kinds of moths flit and fly through the night sky.

Adult butterflies and moths have two pairs of wide wings. And most have long, straw-like mouthparts. But these graceful insects start their lives in a very different way.

Tiny caterpillars hatch from eggs. The little ones gorge and grow, munch and **molt**.

After the insects shed their exoskeletons for the last time, they become **pupae**. Butterflies change inside a **chrysalis**. But moths rearrange their bodies inside a **cocoon**.

After a few days, weeks, or months, the adults break out of their cases. Then they soar off into the sky.

Q: Why didn't the butterfly go to the dance?

A: Because it was a moth ball.

monarch butterfly

Q: What's the biggest moth in the world?

A: A mammoth.

5 Dragonflies and Damselflies

These insects might look delicate. But they're true survivors. In fact, they've lived on Earth for more than 300 million years. And they're some of the fiercest predators around.

When one of these hungry hunters spots an insect, tadpole, or small fish, it grabs the prey with its legs and drags the helpless victim into its mouth—all while still flying!

At rest, an adult dragonfly holds its wings out straight. But a damselfly folds its wings above its back. In flight, these insects have all the right moves. They spend their days snatching mosquitoes and other insects out of the air. Then they devour the prey with strong, chewing mouthparts.

dragonfly

Q: What did the dragonfly call the mosquito?

A: Lunch.

yum...

He called me what?!?

Q: Why was the entomologist a hero?

A: He saved a damselfly in distress.

Bees, Wasps, and Ants

What do these insects have in common? Well, for starters, they can shake their butts. Yup, that's right. Almost all bees, wasps, and ants have a narrow "waist" between their thorax and abdomen. That means they can—and do—wiggle their back ends.

But that's not all. These insects have compound eyes, so they have great eyesight. And most defend themselves by biting or stinging their enemies.

Many bees, wasps, and ants live in large groups called colonies. Each nest has a queen to lay eggs and thousands—even millions—of workers.

Not all of these insects have wings. But the ones that do flap furiously as they fly. The wings make a low, buzzing sound.

Q: What happened when the honeybee called its hive?

A: It got a buzzy signal.

honeybees

Q: What's the biggest kind of ant?

A: A gi-ant.

15

Flies and Mosquitoes

If it's small and it flies, then it must be a fly. Right? Not always.

Flies are a specific group of insects. And believe it or not, mosquitoes belong to the same group. What makes these insects special? They have just one pair of wings. But that doesn't slow them down a bit. In fact, they're the best fliers in the insect world. Many flies can hover, spin, and even fly backward. Wow!

Like other insects, flies begin their lives as eggs. The **larvae** that hatch are called maggots. Maggots chow down on rotting flesh for a few weeks, and then become pupae. Adult flies feed on just about anything you can think of—from plant juices to animal wastes and even human blood. Yuck!

fly

Q: What did the housefly say to the mosquito?

A: Don't bug me.

Q: What does a Mexican frog eat for lunch?

A: A mosquito burrito.

Mosquito Burrito

Q: How do you keep flies out of the kitchen?

A: Put a pile of manure in the living room.

Grasshoppers and Crickets

Boing! Boing! These leggy leapers move across fields and forests in giant jumps. But they're hard to spot when they're sitting still.

One thing's for sure—grasshoppers and crickets really know how to blend in. If a hungry hunter gets too close, a nasty-smelling fluid oozes out of the insects' bodies. One sniff of the stinking stench sends most predators running.

Grasshoppers and crickets have three life stages—egg, **nymph**, and adult. The youngsters look just like their parents—only smaller.

Believe it or not, some grasshopper nymphs eat twice their body weight every single day! No wonder they spend so much time munching and crunching on leaves and stems.

Q: What does a cricket like to do at recess?

A: Jump rope.

Q: What's a grasshopper's favorite day?

grasshopper

A: February 29. Because it only happens during leap year.

Stick Insects and Mantids

stick insect

Bet you can guess what stick insects look like. That's right! Twigs and stems. Their long, slender bodies and spindly legs make them true masters of disguise.

During the day, stick insects stay perfectly still. That way enemies can't spot them. At night, they creep along branches and munch on leaves.

Have you ever seen a praying mantis? It is the most common member of the mantis family. Like a stick insect, a praying mantis is long and thin. And its bright green body blends in perfectly with plants.

But don't be fooled by this cute little critter. Its **camouflage** does more than help it hide. The mantis is a mighty hunter that lies in wait and catches its prey by surprise. Besides insects, it eats lizards, fish, frogs, birds, and small snakes.

Q: What game does a stick insect hate to play?

A: Pickup sticks.

Q: What kind of insect always goes to church?

A: A praying mantis.

10 Termites and Cockroaches

Cockroaches are some of the oldest insects around. They've lived on Earth for at least 300 million years. Scientists think the first termites developed from roaches about 220 million years ago. That's 70 million years before the first butterflies appeared. Wow!

Like bees and ants, termites live together in colonies. When the nymphs hatch, they're helpless. Worker termites feed them. And guard termites protect the whole **colony** from enemies. Only the queen lays eggs.

Cockroaches usually live alone. But they come together when it is time to mate. Each female lays an egg case with up to thirty developing nymphs. She carries it around for almost a month. Finally, she hides the sac in a dark, safe place. Then the nymphs break out and start searching for food.

Q: What do you call a female termite?

A: A her-mite.

termite colony

Q: What kind of bug keeps the peace?

A: A cop-roach.

Fleas and Lice

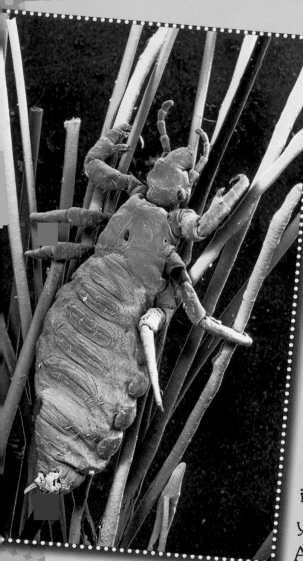

head louse

One thing's for sure. These nasty little bloodsuckers don't make good houseguests. In fact, they can cause a whole lot of trouble for us and our pets.

Fleas don't have wings. But that's no problem. They just jump. If you could jump like a flea, you could leap over a fifty-story building. Fleas attack **warm-blooded** animals with razor-sharp mouthparts. Then they slurp up blood until they're full.

What's a louse's favorite snack? Your skin and blood. The little insect grabs hold of your hair with its tiny claws. Then it slices and dices your skin like an expert chef. As far as lice are concerned, nothing's tastier than YOU.

Q: What's the difference between a puppy and a flea?

A: A dog can have fleas, but fleas can't have puppies.

Q: Where do insects go shopping?

A: At a flea market.

Spiders

How is a spider different from an insect? It has two main body parts—a **cephalothorax** and an abdomen. It also has eight legs. A spider is the only animal with tiny tubelike **spinnerets** on the bottom of its abdomen. They let out silk made inside the spider's body.

Almost all spiders are meat eaters, but they need to liquify their prey before they can eat it. As they bite with their fangs, poisonous **venom** flows into the victim's body. In seconds, the prey is dead or **paralyzed**. Most spiders target insects. But some hunt small fish, birds, and mice.

Think all spiders spin webs? No way! Only about half of all spiders use webs to trap prey. But all spiders use silk to wrap their egg sacs. And most spiders use silk safety lines to escape from enemies.

Q: Why is it so easy to fool a spider?

A: It has eight legs to pull.

common garden spider

Q: Why do spiders spin webs?

A: They don't know how to knit.

27

Daddy Longlegs

What does a daddy longlegs have in common with a spider? Not as much as you might think.

Okay, sure, they both have fat, round bodies. They both have eight legs. But that's about it.

A daddy longlegs has just one main body part—not two. And it only has two eyes—not eight. You'll never guess how a daddy longlegs hears, feels, smells, and tastes. It uses tiny hairs and sensors on its legs.

Like spiders, daddy longlegs eat meat. But they don't inject prey with venom. And they can't trap victims in a web because they don't make silk.

Q: What do you get if you cross a daddy longlegs with an elephant?

A: I'm not sure. But if you see one walking across the ceiling, RUN!

Q: Why did the toad play a trick on the daddy longlegs?

A: It's easy to pull its leg.

Scorpions

Dinosaurs, woolly mammoths, and saber-tooth cats have come and gone. But scorpions just keep on surviving. They've lived on Earth for more than 400 million years.

What makes a scorpion so tough? Its flat, narrow body can fit into most rocky cracks. And the stinger on a scorpion's tail is lethal to prey. Would you believe that some scorpions can lift more than twenty times their body weight with one claw? It's true.

Scorpions can live almost anywhere. You can find them on sandy beaches or snow-covered mountains, in rain forests or caves more than 2,000 feet (610 m) underground.

Female scorpions keep their eggs inside their bodies for up to a year. Then as many as one hundred little scorpions are born at once. The youngsters ride around on their mom's back until they can survive on their own.

Q: What's a scorpion's favorite TV show?

A: Survivor.

Q: Who's a scorpion's favorite musical performer?

A: Sting.

15 Ticks and Mites

tick

What do ticks have in common with Count Dracula? They vant to suck your blood. Ticks cling to tall grass and grab onto any victim that passes by. They usually feed on the blood of birds and mammals. But they aren't too picky. They'll also dine on reptiles and amphibians.

Mites are closely related to ticks, but they aren't bloodsuckers. Many mites live in water or soil. They eat plants or rotting material. But some mites live on animals—including humans. They eat skin cells and body juices.

You probably have itty-bitty mites living in your eyelashes right now. But you need a microscope to see them. They might be crawling around on your nose, forehead, cheeks, or chin! And you could have itch mites living in your armpits or between your fingers. Yuck!

Q: Why was the tick mad at his friend?

A: There was bad blood between them.

Q: How did the mites spend their Saturday night?

A: Dancing cheek to cheek.

Pill Bugs

At first glance, a pill bug might look like a beetle. But take a closer look. A pill bug has fourteen legs.

Some people call this creepy, crawly critter a roly-poly. When it senses danger, it curls up in a tight ball. Its hard exoskeleton acts like a suit of armor. It keeps the pill bug safe.

Pill bugs live in damp places. They rest during the day. At night, they munch on dead leaves.

A female pill bug keeps her eggs inside a pouch on her belly. After the tiny youngsters hatch, they eat and grow, eat and grow all summer long. When autumn comes, they hibernate under leaves on the forest floor. It's a pill bug's life!

Q: What did the pill bug say to his friend when he spotted a bird?

A: Let's roll!

Q: How many pill bugs can you put in an empty can?

A: One. After that, the can isn't empty.

17 Millipedes and Centipedes

Centi- means one hundred. And *ped* means feet. So you might guess that centipedes have a hundred feet, right? But hold on. You can't always trust an animal's name.

Some centipedes really do have about a hundred legs. But most have around fifty. And some have more than three hundred.

A millipede's name is just as confusing. They don't really have a thousand feet. They have between forty and four hundred. Just imagine what they'd look like doing a jig!

Millipedes and centipedes both live in the soil. But they act very differently. Centipedes move fast. They use venom to attack insects and earthworms. Millipedes move much more slowly and eat rotting plants.

millipede

Q: Why don't centipedes play baseball?

A: By the time they put on their cleats, the game is over.

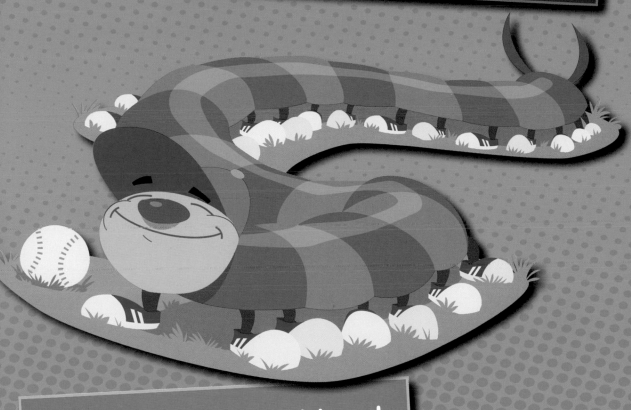

Q: How do you tell which end of a millipede is its head?

A: Tickle its middle and see which end laughs.

How to Write Your Own Jokes

Writing jokes isn't hard if you keep three helpful hints in mind:

1. Try to think of a joke's punch line, or answer, first. Then work backward to come up with the setup, or question.

2. Keep the setup short and simple. People who listen to your joke will want to try to guess the answer. That's half the fun. But if the question is too long, your listeners won't be able to remember it all. They'll feel frustrated instead of excited.

3. Keep the answer short and simple too. That way it will pack more of a punch.

Popular Expressions

Ever heard someone say: "I've got butterflies in my stomach"? It means that person is nervous and has a fluttery feeling in his or her belly.

Can you use this popular expression as the punch line for a joke? You bet!

Some caterpillars become butterflies when they grow up, so here's a question that works perfectly with your punch line:

Q: What happens when you eat caterpillars?

A: You get butterflies in your stomach.

Can you find another joke in this book that uses a popular expression as a punch line? Now try to think of your own joke based on a popular expression.

Homographs and Homophones

A homograph is a word or phrase with two or more different meanings. One example is the word *spot*. It can mean "to see" or "a round mark or stain."

You can create a question that seems to use one definition of a word and an answer that uses the other. Here's an example:

Q: **What did the wasp wear on chilly mornings?**

A: **Its yellow jacket.**

Homophones are two or more words that sound the same, but are spelled differently and have different meanings. For example, *spider* and *spied her* are homophones.

You can create a great joke by mixing homophones. Here's an example:

Q: Why did the fly fly?

A: The spider spied her.

These jokes are fun because your family and friends might be able to guess the answers. And sometimes they'll come up with different answers that are just as good. Then you'll have some brand-new jokes to tell someone else.

You can have lots of fun using homographs and homophones to create jokes that will amuse your friends.

Similar Sounds, Different Meanings

Changing a few little letters can also result in words that sound almost the same, like *lion* and *lying* or *cheetah* and *cheater*. And these word pairs can be the inspiration for some hilarious jokes.

Here's an example:

Q: How do injured insects get to the hospital?

A: In an ant-bulance.

This joke works because *ant* sounds a lot like *am,* but it completely changes the meaning of the word.

Can you think of your own bug joke that uses similar-sounding words to really pack a punch?

Rhyme Time

Playing with words to create rhymes can be highly entertaining. It is even better when a rhyme is the heart of a joke. Here's an example:

Q: What kind of insect gets really stressed out?

A: An uptight termite.

Getting Silly

Sometimes the best jokes are ones that are just plain silly or ridiculous. Get ready to laugh out loud—here are some great examples:

Q: What is the difference between a fly and a bird?

A: A bird can fly but a fly can't bird!

Q: How do you tell which end of a millipede is its head?

A: Tickle its middle and see which end laughs.

Words to Know

abdomen—The back section of an insect's body.

camouflage—The ability of some living things to blend in with their surroundings.

cephalothorax—The front part of a spider's body. It includes the spider's eyes, mouthparts, and legs.

chrysalis—The case or covering in which a butterfly transforms from a larva to an adult.

cocoon—The case or covering in which moths and some other insects transform from a larva to an adult.

colony—A group of animals that live together.

dung—Animal droppings.

entomologist—A scientist who studies insects.

exoskeleton—The hard, protective outer layer that covers the bodies of arthropods.

larva (pl. larvae)—The second stage in the life of amphibians and many arthropods.

molt—To shed an old exoskeleton that is too small.

nymph—The second stage in the life of some insects.

paralyze—To make an animal unable to move.

pupa (pl. pupae)—The third stage in the life of some insects.

species—A group of living things that share certain characteristics and can mate and produce healthy young.

spinneret—A tubelike structure on a spider's abdomen that releases silk.

thorax—The middle section of an insect's body, where the legs are attached.

venom—A poisonous liquid that some animals make inside their bodies.

warm-blooded—Having the same body temperature no matter how warm or cold the surroundings are.

Your Jokes in Print

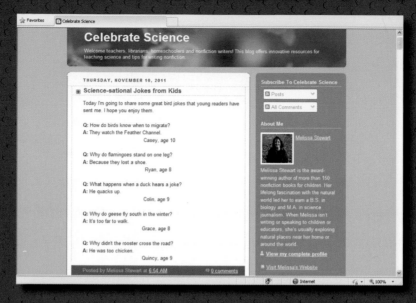

Now it's your turn. See if you can come up with some seriously silly jokes of your own. Then share them with your family and friends. You can submit your most science-sational jokes to:

mas@melissa-stewart.com.

Be sure to include your first name and your age.

The best jokes will be posted on Fridays at:

http://celebratescience.blogspot.com

People all over the world will be able to read and enjoy them. You can send drawings, too. Now get to work on some jokes, and don't forget to have a good time!

Learn More

Books

Latimer, Jonathan P., ed. *Simon & Schuster Thesaurus for Children*. New York: Simon & Schuster, 2001.

Winner, Cherie. *Everything Bug: What Kids Really Want to Know About Bugs*. Minnetonka, Minn.: NorthWord Press, 2004.

Young, Sue. *Scholastic Rhyming Dictionary*. New York: Scholastic, 2006.

Internet Addresses

Bug Guide
<http://bugguide.net/node/view/15740>

insects.org
<http://www.insects.org/>

Index